(M)using ALONG THE IKE

CONTEMPORARY POEMS AND PROSE

NANCY SACK

Outskirts Press, Inc.
Denver, Colorado

The opinions expressed in this manuscript are solely the opinions of the author and do not represent the opinions or thoughts of the publisher. The author has represented and warranted full ownership and/or legal right to publish all the materials in this book.

Musing Along the Ike
Contemporary Poems and Prose
All Rights Reserved.
Copyright © 2010 Nancy Sack
v3.0

Cover Photo © 2010 JupiterImages Corporation. All rights reserved - used with permission.

This book may not be reproduced, transmitted, or stored in whole or in part by any means, including graphic, electronic, or mechanical without the express written consent of the publisher except in the case of brief quotations embodied in critical articles and reviews.

Outskirts Press, Inc.
http://www.outskirtspress.com

ISBN: 978-1-4327-5541-6

Outskirts Press and the "OP" logo are trademarks belonging to Outskirts Press, Inc.

PRINTED IN THE UNITED STATES OF AMERICA

Table of Contents

Poems   1
   A Fifth Generation Funeral Director   3
   A Merry Play   4
   Angry and Hungry   5
   Apache Woman   6
   Beautiful Mary Catherine   7
   Beginnings   9
   The Black Sonata   10
   Blueberry Picking   11
   Books   12
   Charity   13
   City King   14
   Colon-Mindoscopy   15
   Death's Dying Words   16
   Falling   17
   Flight   18
   Flight of the Paper Bag   19
   Forgiveness   20
   Goodness Spills Forth   21
   Growing Round   23
   Hope   24
   If Barbie Were Real   25
   If Everyone Got a Massage   26
   If Only   27
   If Toilets Could Talk   28
   Instant Remedy   29
   Julia   30
   Karaoke Queen   31
   The Lake   32
   Living Clueless   33
   Living with Uncertainty   35
   Loss   36
   Marriage Mirage   37

Moondream	38
Musing Along the Ike	39
My Delight	41
My Request	42
Nature	43
New Life	44
Obama Time Rap	45
Our Annie	46
Pockets	48
Purity	50
Remorse	53
Reuben	54
Ride the Cart	55
Side Effects	57
Sweet Night	58
Swinging	59
The Unwelcome Guest	60
Von Freeman	61
Waiting	62
When You Have No Answers	63
Winter	64
Wyatt Wilson	65
Prose	**67**
The "L"	69
Panera Rage	73
Passing Time	76
Pull Back	79

Poems

A Fifth Generation Funeral Director

I offer an expansive range in costs
and services for all choices.

I am a fifth generation funeral director
and business has never been better.
I offer an array of services
from burial to cremation
or an alternative of your choice.

I am committed to excellence
in serving your family.
I have an array of coffins
and will cater to all kinds of traditions.

Make an appointment today.
I care about your dying family members.

A Merry Play

Let's put on a play
Just you and I
We'll invite the neighbors
I know they'll stop by

We'll have a kingdom
And wear our glitter ring
We'll slay the dragon
And even save the king

The neighbors will be glad
At the end of our show
The king is safe in his castle
And the dragon had to go

Angry and Hungry

The other day
while balancing my cumbersome teaching folders
on my cart
while rushing to class
between the 5 minute passing period
before my 4th period class
wondering if I could make a quick pit stop
in the bathroom
before convening with my 30 students
who are proud of the fact they hate to read
especially those boring works of Shakespeare, Homer, and Dickens
any story longer than three pages is much too long
weaving my cart through the cluttered hallway
my colleague darts by me and says,
there are only two words that end in "gry"—angry and hungry
could this be true? I ponder while scrambling to class
I'd have to check the entire dictionary—no time—not even to pee
as I encounter 30 students blocking my classroom door
hoping to have a sub so they can socialize rather than work
opening my classroom door I'm thinking
I'm angry you've given up or given less of yourself.
I'm hungry for learners.

Apache Woman

I remember

the eyes of the mountain lion
the eyes of the buffalo
the eyes of the fallen deer
the eyes of my dead son

I remember

Beautiful Mary Catherine
(dedicated to those who perished on 9/11)

Beautiful Mary Catherine
Mother of three, young children
Who run to you each day
You arrive home from work

This morning you're ready
For the executive meeting
Your passion fills the room
An events coordinator
Enriching the lives of so many.
Surveying the conference room
Your thoughts turn to Thanksgiving
Only two months away
Traveling with your family to Chicago
Sharing the holiday
With your parents and brothers.

Proposals are placed neatly
On the conference table
Coffee is brewing
You are well-prepared
Your competence exudes calmness.

A thunderous, horrific sound
An explosion, a fiery inferno
Chaos screaming chaos
Your soothing heart
Your helping hands
The elevator crowded to capacity
Crumbling mortar
Crashing
Crashing
Crashing.

Your colleagues cannot find you.
Your children cannot run to you.
Your husband cannot hold you.
Your family cannot be with you.
Mary Catherine
Mary Catherine
Mary Catherine.

Beginnings

Redemption awaits

as the dew spreads across the spring green grass

as the chestnut mare nuzzles her mahogany foal

as the mother draws her newborn to her breast

the future just within her grasp.

The Black Sonata

Black
The rich chocolate cookies
Filled with a golden cream
The ones you shared
With your youngest brother
Only on those special occasions
Because sweets were such a rarity
When shoes needed to be bought
Never forgetting
Those delicious memories of childhood.

Black
Your glistening hair
With its beautiful, sable sheen
Reflecting the radiance
Of the Midnight New Year's Eve Festival
Toasting to a year of new hopes
Never forgetting
Past struggles and sorrows.

Black
Every dress and skirt
You wore for a year
To mourn
Your brother's death
Shot point blank
In a Bosnian café
Over a political argument
Which had no solution
Never forgetting
The blackness of that most lamentable day.

Blueberry Picking

I went blueberry picking
With Laura, Betty, and Mama, too
All day long picking berries
Now my fingers are blue

I ate so many berries
So plumpy, juicy, and sweet
My belly is bursting
They're my favorite treat

Tomorrow's Mama's going to be bakin'
Blueberry muffins, blueberry crisp, and blueberry pie
And by belly will be bursting again
Oh my, oh my, oh my

Books

I love books

Big books
Skinny books
Fancy books

I love
To touch them
To smell them
To hug them

But most of all
I love
To read them

Charity

It's not my problem if my neighbors are getting divorced.
It's not my concern if my mother is lonely.
I send my yearly donation to the United Way.

What can I do with the troubled kid down the block?
What can I do if my friend just lost his job?
I send my yearly donation to the United Way.

I don't have time to visit my relative in the hospital.
I don't have time to talk to a depressed friend.
I send my yearly donation to the United Way.

My eyes grow blind.
My ears grow deaf.

City King

He whirls and twirls the wide sidewalks
calls the city his kingdom
claims the park bench his throne
and he's not to be found at home

Sometimes he sits at the bus stop
with his brown paper bag in hand
other times he rests against the alley wall
with his eyes gazed into the poolroom hall

Sometimes he sways like a ship at sea
and wanders from dock to dock
other times he's still like a cat asleep
and dreams of a treasure to keep

He whirls and twirls the wide sidewalks
calls the city his kingdom
claims the park bench his throne
and he's not to be found at home

Colon-Mindoscopy

Rid the colon
Of polyps, growths, and tumors

Rid the mind
Of shortcomings, failures, and toxic thoughts

Healthy colon
Healthy mind

Death's Dying Words

I am finished with this business of final good-byes.
No more shall I play a role in a person's painful demise.
I will not support those soothing, sugary lies.
Heaven is a beautiful, bountiful paradise.

I'll no longer partake in this ultimate sting.
I quit. That's it.
Don't give me a ring.

Falling

Her familiar name
Falls off my tongue
Like my steady gait
Slips from my grasp
The evening sun
Sinks into the horizon

What's her name
This woman of grace
Her affable smile
Those lines on her face
She closes the door
She's my lost Lenore

Searching searching
So long ago
There's something more
So long ago
I forgot to behold
Lost beyond the horizon

Flight

The little, dark-haired children running
Flying their kites
Letting more of the string go

The children watching their kites
They see no further behind them
Their mothers gazing at their sons
They see a future ahead of them

The string grows taut

Flight of the Paper Bag

Resting now on the chipped, green bench
Feeling wrinkled but comforted
Her life did not end in the land of bin.

With Strong Windgust
She takes flight
Learning of sad human tales.

Pitiful lives wrapping up in themselves
Neglecting to care for the creatures of less
Polluting the earthen roots and waters of blue
Rushing in cars to buildings of work
Living their lives in troubled pursuit
Of newer improved consumer delights.

Soaring higher, surveying Mother Earth
Knowing her soul is too weary
For more travels of woe
She beckons Wise Windgust
To take her to the land of bin.

Forgiveness

The withered
brown leaves
fall from the trees.

Like the failures
of the past
the wind carries them away.

Spring will come
nourishing you with Hope
bringing her gentle rains.

Softly she will open
each delicate petal
of your heart.

Beckoning you
to begin again
to begin again.

Goodness Spills Forth

Rushing to make her connecting flight
from Atlanta to Washington D.C.
she had fifteen minutes to dash
into the washroom for a moment of relief
She'd stop there and forgo
the cramped toilet on the plane

A high-powered consultant traveling
cross-country three times a week
she was used to the frantic movements
of travelers scurrying to their gates
She successfully weaved her way
in and out of hurried walkers
thus making record time to the washroom

She darted into the bathroom
And found an empty cubicle
Wow, no wait! What a miracle!
She now would have a minute on the plane
to get out her book from her travel case
and perhaps finish the conclusion
with calmness for a change

Quickly making her way to the sink to wash her hands
she noticed a petite, white-haired woman
dressed in a pale blue pants suit
crying ever so softly
"Can I help you?" the consultant
approached the petite lady gently
"I am so nervous about flying
and finding my connecting gate
that I've wet myself because I didn't
make it to the bathroom in time"

The consultant could see
the blue slacks stained with urine
"I'll see if I can pick up something for you
to wear in the gift shop"
She consoled the tearful woman

Dashing into the gift shop
The consultant knew she would
No longer make her flight
she asked the clerk if she had any sweats
or slacks for sale in the store
The clerk informed her she only had
Atlanta Braves gym shorts for purchase
Buying a size small pair of guy shorts
The consultant headed back to help
The petite, white-haired lady
get into her Atlanta Braves gym shorts

The consultant led the petite lady
wearing the Atlanta Braves decal
on her derriere to her departing gate
"You may have to become
an Atlanta Braves fan now that
you're sporting the proper attire"
The white-haired lady gleamed
as she waved and exited her gate

The consultant checked the next
departure time for Washington D.C.
She had a three-hour wait
Maybe she would buy a cup of tea
And finish the conclusion of her book

Goodness spills forth….

Growing Round

I'm growing fat, my dear
a baby inside I hear.
Rumbling and flipping around
turning my life upside down.

I'm growing fat, my dear
a June date draws near.
Eating and munching away
perhaps I'll be popping in May.

I'm growing fat, my dear
a duplicate birth I fear.
Rumbling and flipping around
turning my life upside down.

Hope

Our Father
who art in Heaven

Peel away the earth's surface
so I can get a glimpse
of my ninety-year-old Granny
lifting her plum-colored dress
revealing her red satin slip
as she lights across the dance floor

Peel away the earth's surface
so I can feel Uncle Bob's powerful hands
on the piano keys pounding
those joyful Christmas carols

Peel away the earth's surface
so I can thank my biology teacher
for showing me the beauty of cells
under the microscope

Peel away the earth's surface
so I can hug gentle Sis
whose smile and acceptance
always warmed my soul

Peel away the earth's surface
so I can hear Jack's big laugh
as I tell him another silly joke

Peel away the earth's surface
so I can kiss my friend Jeff
who drowned at fifteen breathless
a full future ahead of him

Peel away the earth's surface
so I can taste the sweet morsel
of immortality.

If Barbie Were Real

If Barbie were real
she'd head right over
to the Burger King
and get a whopper with fries.

If Barbie were real
she'd put on a pair of overalls
over her denim work shirt
and go to the movies munching on popcorn.

If Barbie were real
she'd worry about the economy
because her friends can't get jobs
even though they have the qualifications.

If Barbie were real
she'd finally be brave
and tell her parents she doesn't love Ken
because she's gay and has a partner named Faye.

If Everyone Got a Massage

If everyone got a massage
there would be no war

Strip the despotic rulers
of their tyrannical powers
Strip the men and women
of their destructive weapons
Strip the fanatic extremists
of their ruthless missions
Strip the right wing fringe groups
of their supremacist, hateful actions
Strip the ignorant children
of their parent-learned prejudices
that divide brothers and sisters
reducing the world to ashes

Knead out the vengeance
of vicious evil-doers
Knead out the tainted power
of malevolent leaders
Knead out the xenophobia
of narrow-minded people
Knead out the ethnic strife
of religious zealots
Knead out the malicious nationalism
of power-hungry politicians
that divides countries
reducing the world to ashes

If everyone got a massage
there would be no war

If Only

If only I could caress your cheek
and take you away from the flames
of judgment, hatred and ridicule
that scorch your anguished face.

If only I could kiss those troubled lips
and take you among the wheat fields
together embracing the sun's warmth
while the wind carried our sorrows away.

If only I could grasp you from your pain
I would lead you to the lilies
touching your soul with my eyes
protecting your heart from the interlopers.

If Toilets Could Talk

Oh no, here come the wee children with spring in their hearts
in goes the shampoo bottle followed by the bar of soap,
the toilet paper, 9 dimes and mama's new necklace of hope.
Those buggers flushed twice, leaving me to cope.

Oh no, you shouldn't have had 5 hotdogs with onions
followed by 3 pieces of apple pie.
Fireworks and picnics are great traditions, oh my,
but a bottle of Jack Daniel's on the 4th of July?

Oh no, are you crying again?
they'll come visit you, maybe on Christmas Day.
You've been a wonderful mom in your loving way.
I know this nursing home is not a good place to stay.

If the toilets could talk,
perhaps they would demand extra pay.

Instant Remedy

There is an instant remedy for everything
there has to be, you see
because we live in a pre-fab society.

There's instant money, instant jobs,
instant beauty, instant relationships,
and instant knowledge.
Instant remedies to an instant life.

There's quick relief, quick success,
quick love, quick divorce,
 and quick death.
Instant remedies to an instant life.

There is an instant remedy for everything.
there has to be, you see
because we live in a pre-fab society.

Julia

Julia's at the street corner each night
fighting the cold wind's bite
She doesn't stay too long
only to sing her sad song

Julia's mama had ten of her own
her papa was never home
There wasn't much food to be found
until the day the pimp came around

Julia's making good money now
her mama doesn't understand how
Julia calls her profession fashion design
her mama believes it's the work of the Divine

Julia's at the street corner each night
fighting the cold wind's bite
"Oh, Julia, why are you in this mess?"
"Tell me now, can't you guess?"

Karaoke Queen

By day Lynn works at the Osco
re-stocking shampoos, liquid soaps, conditioners
and other beauty products of necessity
She calls her customers honey
and helps everyone who needs assistance
"Aisle Fourteen, honey, for hairbrushes
sixteen for shampoo and hair conditioners
Now you have a good day and stay warm"

By night Lynn sheds her Osco smock
heads over to Riley's
because unbeknownst to the patrons of Osco
Lynn is the Karaoke Queen
singing those passionate songs
of Patsy Cline, Stevie Nicks, Bonnie Raitt,
Sheryl Crow, and Melissa Etheridge
to a crowd of suburbanites
who escaped from their children and pets
for an evening of nostalgic bliss

Her soulful voice enchants her listeners
Lynn, the Karaoke Queen
Tonight, you're our shining star

The Lake

Let's go to the lake
Just you and me

We'll take a dip
Oh, the fish we'll see

Minnows and bass
Trout and perch
They swim really fast
We'll climb the white birch

We'll collect pinecones
Nuts and shiny rocks
We'll bring them all home
And hide them in our socks

Let's go to the lake
Just you and me
You'll have so much fun
Swimming with me

Living Clueless

Mary, talking loudly to Sally in the hallway,
not paying attention
to where her body is taking her,
bumps into Jane, a painfully shy girl,
who steers away from contact at all costs.

Mrs. Smith shouts at Cathy, the bagger,
to give her paper instead of plastic bags,
thinking Cathy, who has Downs Syndrome,
has a hearing problem
when in fact
Cathy's hearing is excellent.

Kevin calls his buddy Joe gay
which means he thinks he's stupid
and doesn't know his best friend Jim
who is sitting next to Kevin at the lunch table
is struggling with gender issues
thinking he may be gay.

Bob, who believes he is superior
in all matters of intellectual thought,
unawaringly destroys
his fragile friendship with John
pontificating his viewpoints
while conveying
condescending unacceptance
of John's opinions.

Clara, the nursing aid,
asks PHD botanist Francis
if she would like
to be wheeled to the recreation room
to watch the fashion show
when in fact
Francis, incapacitated by stroke,
and unable to speak
would rather be wheeled outside
to view the array of flowers
in the garden
than take in a day of fashion
for thirty- year-old, healthy women
with affairs to attend.

Living with Uncertainty

I am certain about this bridge of uncertainty where I live

not married yet not divorced
not despondent yet not contented
not fragmented yet not whole
not settled yet not lost
not a reality yet not a dream

I am certain about the uncertainty of when I can embark from this bridge

searching for the Elysian Fields
the land of milk and honey
the place of the gods
where all are bathed
in Light and Goodness

Loss

The sun heated my cold, wet face
 after a summer swim.
The lamb's hair blanket covered my shivering body
 after a midnight snowball fight.
The blaze in the fireplace thawed out my hands
 after an evening sleigh ride.
The scalding tea with honey soothed my stomach
 after a bout with the flu.
Your brilliant body caressed mine with tenderness
 after I gave up my loneliness.
Today the cold emptiness engulfs me.
Groping for the past
 I can almost hear your warm voice.
Barren, brittle, breaking
Death beckons me.

Marriage Mirage

You will solve all my problems.
You will satisfy me sexually.
You will change me for the better.
You will make me very happy.

You will always agree with me.
You will always understand me.
You will always want me.
You will make me very happy.

You will never argue with me.
You will never fight with me.
You will never want to leave me.
You will make me very happy.

You will think the way I do.
You will believe the way I do.
You will live the way I do.
You will make me very happy.

Am I married?
Maybe next year.

Moondream

Splash a Moonbeam
Over
Me

And I'll eat up all the cotton candy clouds
And I'll hula-hoop with Mary Clare
And I'll paint a picture of a purple rose
And I'll run my fingers through Bobby's hair
And I'll swim like a seal in the big blue sea
And I'll climb clear out of my familiar skin
And I'll finally be free so very free

Splash a Moonbeam
Over
Me

Musing Along the Ike

Stuck in traffic on the Ike
My car inches up like a tired, old snail
My thoughts begin to wander
Hoping my engine won't fail

Just another day
Musing along the Ike

Going home from school
This late afternoon
Hot, balmy day
On the first of June

My students have stored
Their brains away
Summer's so near
They're ready to play

My windows are down
Morrison's singing a tune
I'm wishing it were
The tenth of June

The students are itching
To be through with school
I'd rather be dipping
In the local pool

Big Daddy's next to me
Sporting a hairy tattoo
Sitting on his red Harley
Looks brand new

Big Mama's behind him
With her golden tank top
Her bleached blonde hair
Frizzed at the top

Zeppelin's "Stairway to Heaven"
Is cranked up high
Where are they going
Not afraid to die

Daddy's revving his engine
Mama's singing the song
I've stared at them
A second too long

Glancing the other way
But before I do
Mama's given me the finger
And I'm feeling blue

Not sure what to do
Stuck in this jam
I say to Big Mama
"Thank you ma'am"

Hoping for a white stallion
To ride away
Into the sunset
And conclude this day

My Delight

Oh, my Sweet Pea
Come to me

I'll make you fly
Like a butterfly

I'll give you a star
From the heavens afar

I'll take you within
And tickle your skin

I'll open the Iron Gate
And then we'll greet Fate

Oh, My Sweet Pea
Come to me

My Request

Would you paint my portrait?
Can you create an oxymoron?
What colors would you use
to express my duality?
How would you draw the sadness
in my heart over past regrets?
How would you paint the joyous delight
of my new-found discoveries?
Could you make my eyes resonate
the warmth of my family and friends?
Would you gently draw the lines on my face
tracing my joys, sorrows, and longings?
Could you depict the kindness in my soul for all eternity?

Nature

I love to watch the ants
Build a house of dirt

I love to watch the bees
Hover and flirt

I love to watch the spider
Weave a silken skirt

New Life

Mopping up the deluge of tears
Packing up those turbulent years
Throwing them away
No more recycled fears

Shedding the victim role
Gathering up the joy you stole
Re-claiming myself
Finally feeling whole

Splashing color everywhere I go
Green, gold, terracotta, and indigo
Brightening others' lives
 I'm just beginning my show

Deciding to stay
Basking in the moment of the day
I'll live to love
And won't engage any other way

Obama Time Rap

I say good-bye to '08
It wasn't so great
Foreclosures, Depression
Economic Recession
Too many children to feed
Too much corporate greed
No money to spend
The Iraq War must end
I say hello to '09
I'll use Obama's line
"Yes, we can" this time
We must embrace that chime
Practice fiscal responsibility
Nurture all children's ability
Protect our environment
Support global development
Give up the US monologue
Engage in the dialogue
It's Obama's Time
Let's repeat the chime
"Yes, we can"
"Yes, we can"
"Yes, we can"
Hello '09
I'm feeling fine

Our Annie

Her swan-like body
Glides through the water
Shimmering as she swims
Toward the two children
Entrusted under her care
Embracing them with her joy

Gently she rests her chin
Against the mahogany violin
Her deep ebony eyes intense
Playing the Bach composition beautifully
As her black satin hair
Radiates the brilliance of her talent

At seventeen, she discusses
Her college options with her mother
The two together forging her future
A top honors student with infinite possibilities
Planning to study pre-law at Stanford
Her mother shines with pride and contentment

Before the start of her senior year
She climbs into her bed late
Past the midnight hour
After discussing college plans with her mother
Dreaming of her promising future
Hoping to make great contributions

This auburn, dew-filled morning
The angels visit the Daughter of Gentle Grace
Escorting her to Eternal Life
To brighten the heavens above
Too good for this world
An iridescent light of the future

Now our tears nourish the earth
As the yellow orchids adorn your grave.

Pockets

His mom found the chocolate kiss
 from Colleen, a first grade friend,
with the tin foil pressed hard
 against the melted chocolate
deep within his pants pocket
How would he know seven years later
Colleen would be hit by a brown station wagon
while riding her bike and be killed instantly
If only he could hold on to that chocolate
perfection in a kiss
before it melted deep within his pocket.

He stuck his hand in the pockets
of his bomber jacket
as he waited for the school bus
that chilly Monday morning
He pulled out the Bulls' ticket stub
of Saturday night's game
which reminded him of the good time
he had with his dad, mom, and brother
How would he know that six years later
his parents would divorce as empty nesters
because they had nothing in common
once the children were grown
If only he could hold on to that ticket stub
placing it deep within his pocket
so it would never be discarded
as insignificant trash.

He carefully surveyed his mother's closet
a colorful array of silk dresses, wool blazers,
fall sweaters, and pastel linens
He put his hand into the pocket
of his mom's favorite Irish sweater
and there he found the dainty, white handkerchief
embroidered with pink roses
a gift he had given her two summers ago
How would he know his mother
a woman of such grace, civility, and beauty
would be taken from him so abruptly
cardiac arrest the doctor said
Now he can only hold on
to his mother's handkerchief
and place it deep within the pocket of his heart.

Purity

Reading her father's
award-winning poetry
about Vietnam
to her English class
she hears the rain
patter against the window pane

Seeing her father as a young man
rushing across the rice paddies
the monsoon rains
soaking his uniform
the sweat drips off his face

Continuing to read
The Echoes of Vietnam
she sees herself, a girl of eight
peer through the tear-stained window
watching her rain-soaked father
dash to his waiting car

Remembering a teenage shopping spree
she sees her father only for a moment
peel through the puddles of the intersection
in a red truck glistened by the rain

Wondering why her father
left three daughters and a wife
years ago never to see them
grow wise and strong and old

Forgiving her father
for his eternal departure
honoring him twenty years later
as she reads his poetry to her class
one rain-filled day in November

Reflections

I sit down once again
leaning my tired back
against the white stucco wall
supporting the dark roof of my home

My frame rests on my back porch
as I look at the Van Gogh evergreens
slanting inward creating an arch
to a garden of tomatoes and zucchini

As I peer into the cup of my re-heated coffee
I carefully lift the curdled film
from the top trying
not to scald my fingertips

I taste the burnt coffee
realizing I re-heated
that single cup
once too much

I think how many times
I have re-heated
my important issues
once too much

The messy bedroom
the lack of communication
the dirty toilet including the seat
the dishes that won't be put away

Shall I re-heat these issues of mine?
No, not today
as the sun warms my face
as the tomatoes turn red
as the Van Gogh evergreens embrace
as the birds sing their sweet symphony

I shall throw away my issues
into the abyss where trifles are lost
and brew a fresh pot of coffee

Remorse

Rain falling on parched fields
crippled crops eat lifeless land.

People dying with hungry eyes
bloated bellies fill empty hearts.

Thunder calling the barren seed
too late, too late, too late.

Reuben

Oh Reuben, oh Reuben
will you ever go home?
Your lover is waiting
your mother's in tears
and Reuben continues to roam.

Reuben left a long time ago
to find his golden rainbow .
He searched and he searched
 in the West and the East
and still wondered where he should go.

Reuben tried the Far East
and sailed to Bombay,
to drift for over a year.
He spent all his fine money
and was still discontent with his way.

Then he hitched a ride with a merchant
who told him to go to Greece
because Athens was the place to be.
So he worked hard for a plane fare
and flew off to find his longed for peace.

Reuben was enchanted with Greece,
but he had no money of his own.
So he took a job as a fisherman
to court the temperamental sea
and soon forgot his lover at home.

Oh Reuben, oh Reuben
will you ever go home?
Your lover is waiting
your mother's in tears
and Reuben continues to roam.

Ride the Cart

I go to the grocery store
once, twice, maybe three times a week.
I know the contents of the aisles by heart.
Aisle 4 Cereal. Aisle 5 Breads, bagels, and buns.

Today I make my way up and down the aisles
knowing that I have to feed my family.
When I finish, I maneuver my way to the checkout line.
I'm wondering why so many people are buying groceries.
I'm pausing a second, thinking maybe, just maybe
They have to feed their families, too.

Suddenly, I'm gently bumped from behind
By a lady with a cart who thought
my pause was a bit too long.
I inch up noting I only have
ten people in front of me
and contemplate how there are nine check-out stations
but only two checkers today.

Perhaps one of them won the lotto
and took the crew of employees
on a cruise to the Virgin Islands.
I'm wishing I were a friend of that fortunate grocery employee.

So these two checkers must be new
and that's why they are having a difficult time
scanning labels of the grocery items.
I'm feeling bad for these neophytes
because the ladies with their weary children
are in a hurry today as they tap their polished nails
in a machine-gun-like fashion on the cart handles.

I'm thinking now as I'm waiting in line that banks,
social security offices, driver's license centers, and grocery stores
are good places to help people acquire patience.
I need more patience so I decide to recall another time
when I had to stand in a longer line than this one.
I remember the incident last May
at the driver's license center to renew my license
only to discover after two hours of waiting
that my license had not expired.

Wow, it's my turn already.
I've had time to think about virtues, travels, and good fortunes.
I think I'll smile at this young checker
who looks tired and a bit overwhelmed.
I thank him after he has bagged my groceries.
The baggers must be in the Virgin Islands, too.

I make my way to the exit and now is my favorite part
of my weekly outings to the grocery store.
At full speed in the parking lot, I run
pushing my cart full of groceries
and I hop on riding the cart
all the way to my car.

Ride the cart.
Ride the cart.
Ride the cart.

Side Effects

Reading the label
in tiny fine print
of the medicine available
to cure my mom's illness

May cause vomiting, diarrhea,
dementia, peeling skin, hives,
lethargy, excessive cough,
swelling of the feet and legs,
marked drowsiness, dizziness,
nervousness, sleeplessness,
dehydration and excitability.

Worrying over
the last sentence
in tiny print
to cure my mom's condition

If any of these symptoms occur
discontinue use
and consult your doctor.

Wondering if the side effects
are worse than her illness.

Sweet Night

Come Night
Shield me
from hatred, scorn and derision

Come Night
Protect me
from judgment, cruelty and rejection

Come Night
Comfort me
With empathy, kindness and tranquility

A tender repose
From my weariness

Swinging

Two swings in the playground
Reserved for you and me
Let's go swinging together
As high as the big, oak tree

Pump pump pump pump
But don't let go
You can swing high
And you can swing low

Let's swing all day long
'Til the sun waves good-bye
Just you and me
Swinging so high

The Unwelcome Guest

Clandestinely
Unexpectedly
Cancer creeps into my life.

Invading
Weakening
The sturdy walls of my home.

Cracking
Destroying
My solid foundation.

Dear Unwelcome Guest,
Did you know I planted my soul in my children
and have given my courage to my loved ones?
These treasures you cannot take from me.

Von Freeman

Von Freeman, a legendary saxophonist
of scope and soul
whose notes burst forth
in gold, yellow, brown, blue
orange, red, green and purple
deep in hue
expressing joy, beauty, pain, love,
perseverance, forgiveness and redemption

Von Freeman, a legendary jazz musician
of depth and passion
whose creative arrangements
have inspired the young
to wait in line and play for the Mentor
and whose majestic melodies
have awakened the hearts
of his listeners who long to rise
from the ordinariness of their lives
and experience the magic of jazz

Von Freeman, a legendary artist
of warmth and compassion
whose kindness and love of life
have taught me to value
friendship, goodness, beauty,
creativity and individuality

In his own words
"Express yourself, darling."

Thank you, Von Freeman.

Waiting

The other day I spent
what seemed to be an eternity
waiting on hold for a human voice
but I heard the automated voice
of the computer programmed
not to respond to human concerns
of trying to schedule an appointment
for Mom whose heart needs surgery
or of trying to locate a friend at work
whose heart needs mending
from a troubled, difficult relationship
or of trying to locate a parent
so that we can help her child learn to read
only to discover the taped message
please leave your name and phone number
after the beep
beep.

When You Have No Answers

…life can be so beautiful
in the moments…

... when you have no answers,
but beauty and brokenness
that caress
the intimate details
of lives intertwined
with genuine kindness
that reaches far within
the marrow of the bones
that seeks
to dance
to interlace
to live
in the beauty
of the moment….

Winter

Icicles crackling off the burdened roof
boots crunching the hardened snow
birch trees stooping from the gusty gale
a grey sky looming for its defenseless prey
woolen scarves wrapped around timid necks
a harsh wind rushing into teary eyes
winter howling
freezing hopes of warmth.

Wyatt Wilson

When will Wyatt Wilson stop his whining?

Not in kindergarten
Poor Wyatt Wilson
didn't get the blue mat
during story times.

Not in grade school
Poor Wyatt Wilson
didn't want to do homework
because he enjoyed watching TV more.

Not in high school
Poor Wyatt Wilson
didn't want to attend academic classes
only the computer was worth his while.

Not in adulthood
Poor Wyatt Wilson
didn't keep any job he was able to obtain
because work was boring and tedious.

Not in old age
Poor Wyatt Wilson
didn't like his nursing home
because the care was inadequate.

When will Wyatt Wilson stop his whining?

When he dies.

Prose

The "L"

I'm on the Howard L traveling down to Fullerton minding my own business, of course. I'm looking at my baseball cards. Ryne Sandberg, Rick Sutcliffe, Mark Grace, Andre Dawson. I'm thinking these cards could be valuable someday. The Cubbies could be good this year. Morse Stop comes up and before I know it, coming up the platform is a huge, massive lady. Then I do a double-take. This lady, I mean this guy, who thinks
he's a woman, is walking down my aisle looking at the empty seat across from me.

Well, there go my baseball cards all over the floor. I'm picking them up pretty fast now because she's waiting for me to get up. She sits down, glares at me, and straightens her red, shiny, sequined dress. I feel my face getting redder than her dress. Now I'm feeling real hot like I'm sitting in church. I go back to shuffling my baseball cards, but I just can't help staring. I never saw so many sequins on one dress. And those biceps, she makes Rick Sutcliffe look small.

She catches me staring and gives me a stare that says she'll eat me for dinner if I don't fix my eyes elsewhere. She's something else. I can't help staring. Her legs, she's wearing nylons, are full of muscles, but big like elephant's. And her red, sequined dress bulges in all the wrong places. Her neck is a big as a Mack truck. She's got on this platinum, blonde wig which almost fools me until I see it move. Her red lips are thick like rubbery tires. On the side of her mouth is a long, white scar. He looks like a real Mean Doll. The Bears could use her on defense. Even Mike Singletary wouldn't mess with her.

She glares at me again. I bet she knows what I'm thinking. She could crush me in a minute flat. Loyola Stop next. I got 12 stops to go. I'm hoping Mean Doll will get off. No such luck. She keeps glaring at me. I'm glad I've got my baseball cards. By now, I've got them all memorized.

In walks a man about 50 in a three-piece suit and sits across from me next to Mean Doll. I say to myself this could be trouble. He gives Doll a glance, a quick glance, not like my stare, and he shifts a bit closer. First the man turns white like cottage cheese then red like ketchup. Granville Stop. He bolts for the door. I guess he only needs to go one stop. I usually walk if it's only one stop, but he must be in a hurry.

Mean Doll smiles and opens her purse. She's looking for something. She pulls out this red nail polish. I'm staring; we're bumping and stopping--I'm wondering how she's going to polish those big nails. She just finishes shaking, her nail polish that is, when up comes Bryn Mawr Stop. It's getting crowded; I'm thinking more trouble ahead. A businessman, this one's younger, tall and dark. I see the Doll's eyes light up. He sits down beside her. He's reading his paper and doesn't know he's sitting next to Mean Doll. I try to warn him with my eyes, but the Doll catches me and glares. I go back to my cards, but I'm taking it all in.

Doll puts her nail polish away and pulls out a cigarette. "You have a light?" she says to the guy. He looks up at her. He looks like an ant next to Doll. He shakes his head and jumps for the door like a scared jack rabbit. Lawrence Avenue. Out he goes.

In comes an old gray-haired lady carrying an umbrella and wearing a large, straw Jamaica shoulder bag. She sits down next to Doll. She smiles at me. She's kind of old, but she's got a nice smile. She sets her bag down in front of her small feet. She's wearing these black, shiny boots and this pink raincoat. I can't figure her out. It's so hot and sunny I had to wear my Cubs hat. I guess she just really likes her raincoat even though it's pretty wrinkled. But she's smoothing it down and down and down. I'm wondering when she's going to stop. She keeps doing it for the longest time. Then she folds her hands in her lap.

Now I'm wondering if Mean Doll is going to harass this old lady. He's been glaring at her the whole time. Doll keeps watching the old lady perk her neck up just so and bat her eye lashes. She's fluttering at all the people and smiling as wide as a giraffe. Then she turns to me and bats those eyes. I smile a little, but I'm pretending to be studying my cards. You'd think I was cramming for a math test.

Next the old lady with her neck perked up like an ostrich flutters her eyes at Doll and smiles. Doll glares at the old lady. The old lady is still smiling at Doll. "You have a problem?" Doll says to the old lady. Now Doll is really glaring at her. Now I'm feeling bad for the old lady. She's irritating Mean Doll, and she shouldn't be messing with him. But she just keeps smiling at Doll.

"Now listen, lady, you'd better stop smiling like that, or you're going to wish you'd never sat down here." Doll's getting hot. And I'm wondering how I'm going to keep him from hitting the old lady. I could make a run for it, but I'm pretty much cornered in my seat.

But the old lady is still smiling, and then I can't believe what she does. She pats Doll's knee with her wrinkled hand. This is it! The old lady's dead meat. But before Doll has time to do anything, the lady says, "Dear, I'm so sorry I was staring at you, but you remind me of my niece, Wilamena."

I can't believe it. I push my Cubs hat up off my forehead. I got to see if Doll's going to clobber the old lady. She's so little next to Doll. I'm not sure what I'll do if the old lady gets clobbered. Doll would wipe me out with one blow.

Doll is still glaring at the old lady. Then she crosses her legs and slides real close to the old lady. I'm thinking Doll is still hot, but it looks like he's going to give the old lady a chance.

The old lady smiles wide and says, "Now dear," I'm glad she's speaking loud to Doll because I don't want to miss anything. "Wilamena and you have those same big, brown, sensitive eyes." The old lady pats Doll's knee again. I can't believe what I see next. Doll's not glaring anymore. He's smiling at the old lady. "And you both have beautiful smiles," the old lady says.

I'm kind of in shock. Then Doll pats the old lady's knee and says, "Thank you. You're so sweet."

"Oh, Wilamena is the sweet one," the old lady says. "I bet you're as sweet. She visits me at least twice a year. We sit at Jerome's all afternoon and drink wine. We talk about my garden. And we talk about her pets. She has so many pets. The lady smiles. Snakes are her favorite. But she also has a fondness for lizards."

I can't believe what I'm hearing. This lady must be putting Doll on. But Doll's taking it all in, smiling, and nodding. He's loving the conversation. He's telling her about all these different types of snakes and lizards he saw in the San Diego Zoo last year. I can't believe it.

They're talking now like my best buddy, Jimmy, and me. Doll pats the lady's hand. "You know," he says, "I have four cats. And I'm so attached to them. I wouldn't know what to do if something happened to one of them."

The old lady's stretching her neck and fluttering her eyes at Doll. She pats Doll's knee and says, "Don't worry, dear, your cats will be fine. You seem so sensitive. Just like Wilamena. Men look for sensitive women. I keep telling Wilamena that her knight is just around the corner. Don't be too hasty I tell her. She's only 40. Be particular, I tell her."

I can't believe how much the old lady's batting those eyelids. She's batting those eyes and smoothing her raincoat. Belmont Stop. I'm leaning closer, but I got to get off soon.

Doll's talking now. "Well, you know, my cats are just like people. They are all so different. So unique with their personalities and moods."

Now I'm watching Doll. I can't believe what I'm seeing. He's acting just like the old lady, smoothing his dress and fluttering his eyes. Well, the two of them really look like a trip. I'm waiting for Doll to stretch his neck the way the old lady does right before she's about to say something. Sure enough, he's perking it up just like the old lady. I want to start laughing, but I know Doll would kill me if he saw me.

The lady's smiling now. She's got more to say. She's talking to Doll like he's her best friend. "That's what Wilamena says about her snakes. I'm meeting her at the zoo today before we go to Jerome's. She's going to tell me all about the animals there."

Doll smiles at the old lady. Then he flutters his eyes and says, "That's your next stop. Fullerton."

"Oh, thank you, dear. I was enjoying our conversation so I almost missed my stop. Wait until I tell Wilamena about you. You could be sisters."

Fullerton Stop. I let the old lady go in front of me. Doll stands and gives the old lady a kiss on the cheek. Her cheek's all red from Doll's lipstick, but she's beaming now. Doll sits back down and gives me a glare.

I'm kind of worried Doll's going to kick me one because I was staring so. But I pass by with no trouble. I get to the door and turn for one last glimpse of Mean Doll. Doll sees me, smiles, and blows me a kiss. Out I go matching the red C in my Cubs hat.

Panera Rage

Last week after teaching my morning classes,
I drove over to Panera with anticipation
of ordering a tuna fish sandwich on multi-grain bread
with all the extra trimmings minus the mustard
for my friend, Barb, who was recovering from back surgery.
I wanted to spend a couple of hours with my dear friend
before I had to get home for my afternoon session
of errands, practice schedules, play-dates,
snacks, and homework time with my children.

As I drove into Panera's parking lot,
I noticed many cars awaited
their owners' return and consequently
I had to park a good distance away.
I realized that I would have to wait
in line for quite some time so that I could purchase
that delectable treat for Barb whose kindness
parallels the late Mother Teresa.
Yes, I would wait in line for that tantalizing,
tuna fish sandwich on multi-grain bread
with all the trimmings minus the mustard.

As I scurried across the parking lot
and opened the door leading into Panera,
I began my yoga breathing
as I found my place in the back of the long line.
Listening to the customers recite their orders,
my yoga breathing was working well,
when all of the sudden, a woman in a green van
screeches to a dead stop in front of Panera,
gets out of the van, slams the door, and
barges into the restaurant carrying a Panera bag
with a single purpose burning in her heart.

"Get me the manager. I can't believe this place.
I ordered two bread bowls and a salad.
I only got the salad. I want my Panera bread bowls now."
This lady was screaming at the Panera employee
who apologized to the next customer in line
and quickly left her station to get the manager.

When the manager arrived on the scene,
she heard the irate woman's complaints,
and asked for her receipt, checked the order,
gave the lady her Panera bread bowls,
and apologized for the inconvenience.
As the lady stormed out of the restaurant,
she swore she would never return.
The manager checked the receipt once more
and incredulously discovered the receipt
was dated, a week old.
With furor in her heart, the manager
exploded out the front door
to nab the Deceitful Lady
peeling out of the parking lot
with her stolen Panera bread bowls.

Down-trodden, the manager came back
into the restaurant and went back to work
while my cashier began taking orders again.
When my turn arrived, I ordered the tuna fish sandwich
on multi-grain bread with all the trimmings
minus the mustard and minus the yoga breathing.
Still overcome by the Deceitful Lady's behavior,
I followed the customer in front of me
to the next line to pick up my order.
When the Panera employee gave me
my carryout bag, I thanked him
and hurried to my waiting car,
realizing that the Panera fiasco had eaten up
thirty minutes of my time with Barb.

Once I arrived at Barb's house,
I apologized profusely for being so late

and explained the Panera Rage experience to her.
Then I told Barb to sit down and get ready
for a delicious tuna fish sandwich on multi-grain bread
with all the trimmings minus the mustard as I
carefully took the wrapper off of her coveted sandwich.
To my utter dismay, a roast beef with cheese and
lettuce on a baguette smirkingly stared at me.

"You know, I'm in the mood
for roast beef and cheese," Barb giggled.

Passing Time

"Bless me, Father, for I have sinned. I have been late about 10,000 times in the last month."

My priest replies, "Nancy, you know tardiness is one of the seven deadly sins in America. You need to repent and be late no more."

"I will, Father. I know what a terrible sin being late is. The repercussions of my sin have been grave."

As I finish saying my penance at the altar, I make a new vow to myself, that starting today I'm going to be on time. Then I look at my watch and realize that I'm already fifteen minutes late for a dinner engagement.

Why is it that I can't be on time? Something always comes up. I'm getting ready for a friend's wedding. I'm hurrying, nylons on, looking for my slip, with my hair still wet from the shower. I'm thinking I'd better get this hair dried quickly because the Kennedy will probably be packed with cars heading to Wrigley Field to see the Cubs' game.

But I think I've given myself plenty of extra time to get down to St. John's on the North Side. I'm really looking forward to the ceremony. But where is that slip? As I'm groping through my underwear drawer looking for that slip, I hear the phone ring, once, twice…

I don't have the time, but I go running into the living room, half-dressed, past the open-draped window and grab the phone on the fourth ring. Yes, I'm still one of those individuals who pays Comcast for the use of a land phone.

"Hello."

"Nance, it's Mary."

"Mary, how are you doing?" It's great to hear her voice. Wished she hadn't moved to Kansas City after her wedding, but Joe got a great job offer. I sure miss her.

"Okay," she says.

I read her tone. She feels like hell.

"What's wrong?"

"It's Joe and me."

"What do you mean?" Oh no, Joe and Mary, my stomach tightens up, a great couple. She really needs to talk, and I have my friend's wedding. Maybe she only needs a half hour. I could make the wedding in time.

Forty-five minutes later, I hang up the phone, and I'm going to be late once again. But what could I do? Listen Mary, can I put you on hold because I have to go to a wedding? I know you'll understand, and we'll talk about your pending divorce tomorrow.

No, I can't say that. Instead, I listen to her and consequently miss half the wedding despite my driving down the Kennedy at 75 mph, weaving in and out, trying to get to St. John's ten minutes late rather than twenty minutes late. Failed again, and I never even spent the time to find my slip, put on my make-up, or blow dry my hair. I feel horrible sneaking into church, sliding into the back pew which echoes late, late, late.

Something always comes up. I'm walking to my next hour freshman English class with three minutes to spare. Before I started teaching, I always imagined walking leisurely to my next class, accompanied by eager students who desired additional insights on Shakespeare's characterizations and universal themes in Julius Caesar. When faced with reality, I soon learned that I couldn't pontificate on Shakespeare's works during a five-minute passing period. I also learned to skip going to the bathroom between classes because punctuality must take priority over relief.

As it happens, I'm rushing to class, pass the bathroom, but don't enter. I'm thinking about how I'm going to make The Odyssey an exciting piece of literature to my ninth graders who would rather talk about **Kayne West, John Mayer,** and **the Dave Matthews Band**. Suddenly, I'm interrupted by my Princeton-bound editor who never makes a deadline.

"Mrs. Sack, could I talk to you for a minute? It's really important." Paul's intensity could provide enough electricity for Chicago including the metropolitan area.

"Paul, is it really important? I've got to get to class." Sometimes I really get angry that I can't stop and talk to a student for fear of being late to class. But I know the seconds are flying by.

"I just need a minute to explain this form from Princeton."

With two minutes to spare, I stop to listen. "Okay, Paul, but hurry."

"Okay, Mrs. Sack, I feel really bad, but you have to postmark this by tomorrow. I was doing my AP chemistry project, my article for the newspaper, my term paper, and I totally forgot to get this recommendation to you."

"What specifics do they want?" I'm angry with Paul because he's so late with this application form. And now he's going to make me late for class. But I love his enthusiasm, his involvement, and his concern for others. Four years with the newspaper, and he's done an excellent job. And of course, how can I chide him when he reminds me of myself, my weakness, being late?

Paul hurries through his spiel about this Princeton form. I am to write a thorough account of his character which should include his contributions to the school newspaper, postmark it tomorrow, and be on call for their reply. No problem. As I take the form and accept his apology for not getting it to me sooner, the bell rings.

Once again, I'm late running frantically down the hallway while my students mill around my locked classroom.

"Bless me, Principal, for I have sinned. I have been late to class about 10,000 times in the last semester."

My principal replies, "Nancy, don't you know punctuality is the most important objective to attain, implement, and enforce as a teacher? You need to repent and be late no more."

"I will, Principal. The repercussions of my sin have been great."

As I sit in silence, waiting to be absolved by my principal, I hear that familiar, loathsome sound above his desk. I hear its ticking, and my stomach starts to churn. Those awful hands keep moving, and I'm always a good mile behind.

Pull Back

Two weeks ago in a heightened, orange terror alert, Mary and her daughter, Grace, boarded a jet from O'Hare bound for Las Vegas for their yearly trip to see shows, to people watch, and to gamble. Prior to their excursion, Mary had been hospitalized due to her ongoing heart problems. Mary had had two previous heart procedures to attend to the blockage in her arteries. Although Mary had to use an oxygen device, she wasn't going to let this complication detain her from going to Vegas with her daughter during the holiday season.

As she sat next to her daughter, Mary wondered how many more Vegas trips she would be able to take with her daughter. She hoped many more. The dinners and the shows entertained her immensely. The glitter and the colorful array of outfits enchanted her. The clinking and ringing of the slots got her blood flowing. However, these pleasures were minor ones. Her greatest joy was being with her daughter, Grace—hearing her infectious laugh at the comedy shows, watching her green eyes crinkle with contentment over dinner, seeing her arms raised above her shoulders elated by her blackjack hand. Each year she loved spending five, uninterrupted days with her daughter, sharing their lives in simple joys unimpeded by work, volunteer responsibilities, and health issues.

This last time in the hospital, Mary was thankful she only had to stay a week, and surgery was unnecessary for the meantime. During her stay, her daughter had visited her every day telling her about the events of her teaching day. Mary was proud of her daughter. After twenty years of teaching Spanish, Grace had attained her ESL certification to venture on new territory, teaching immigrants English and the culture of the United States. Her mother knew Grace spent long hours preparing materials for her new classes. She knew how dedicated she was to her students. She wanted to teach them the language and the culture of the US so they could succeed. She wanted to teach them to read well, a life-long passion of hers. She took her students to restaurants so they could practice their English. She taught them the rules of baseball and football. She even taught them how to sing "Take Me Out to the Ballgame" for the Seventh Inning Stretch. She had Halloween and Thanksgiving celebrations in her classroom. Mary was so proud when Grace took her students to the Chicago Art Institute where she volunteered as a docent. There she shared her love of art with her daughter's students, teaching them about Monet, Renoir, Degas, Van Gogh, Picasso, and O'Keefe.

Mary was proud of her daughter, Grace. She had had her heartbreaks, but she didn't close the door to new relationships. Mary liked her daughter's new boyfriend, Tony. They had been together a couple of years now, and her daughter was happy. Happiness is what she wanted for her. Mary took a deep breath. Breathing was more difficult for her these days. She hoped she wouldn't have to use her oxygen device on this trip. Sometimes, the walk from one hotel to the next was arduous, but she could still manage. She had been managing for a long time.

Her mother smiled as she watched her daughter reading her novel beside her. Her daughter had a zest for life, for learning, for people, for joy. She was not afraid to take risks. Her daughter was not deterred by disappointment and catastrophe. Mary recalled last winter when three deer darted in front of Grace's brand new Camry, and one of them didn't make it, damaging Grace's car beyond repair. Grace was thankful none of her passengers or herself was hurt. She even expressed concerns to the police officer that she believed the injured deer had run off in the woods and would need immediate attention. Mary had remembered that Grace was unafraid by the deer experience, immediately getting back to driving and living, once again. Her daughter had turned a negative into a positive by expressing her good fortune of being alive. Mary also recalled Grace moving on after a relationship of fifteen years had ended. "His loss." Mary remembered her daughter's words without any bitterness or regret.

Mary felt the joy surge in her veins as the plane landed on the tarmac. She and Grace found their shuttle bus to the Flamingo Hotel, and their adventure was about to begin. They had a quick bite in their hotel, and they decided that they would play the slots in the Flamingo. After playing the slots for an hour and losing about thirty dollars between them, Grace suggested that they go over to the Mirage.

"Are you up for a walk?" Grace asked.

"Of course," Mary replied. "It's no problem. I'm feeling good." Mary was feeling fatigued, but she did not want the evening to end.

"Mom, we can call it a day and go to the Mirage tomorrow. We have five days."

Mary thought a minute about her daughter's suggestion. She remembered the first heart attack—the freight train in her chest, the sirens screaming to the hospital. She wasn't sure she would make it that day.

"Let's go now," she said.

Mary labored a bit on her walk to the Mirage. However, she knew she would be all right if she took her time. The warm breeze felt good against her face. Each year, she relished her temporary escape from the Chicago winter.

As they entered the Mirage, Grace directed her to the slot machines. "I'll meet you back here, Mom. I'm going to look around and try something new," Grace said.

Her daughter knew Mary loved the slots. Sometimes, she won, but she didn't care too much about winning. She loved the atmosphere, the energy, the people. She felt alive in the lobby of the Mirage.

"Sure, honey. Have fun. I'll see you in a little while," Mary said.

Mary found a quarter slot machine and began feeding her coins into the machine. Life had been good to her. Yes, she had had her losses. Due to her husband's early death, she had to raise three children by herself. She remembered those days. She couldn't let herself be afraid. No, not for the children. She worked longer hours and then came home tired only to help with homework, make dinner, do laundry, and then fall into bed hoping morning wouldn't come too soon. The routine turned to years, to a decade. But, she had done a good job she reminded herself. A son and a daughter, both married, living in Atlanta. Now, she had a grandchild. And then, there was Grace—her daughter, her traveling companion, her nurse, her friend, and her soulmate. Yes, she was fortunate, a very lucky woman.

As she placed her tenth coin in the slot machine and pulled the lever, Mary heard a deafening cacophony in the distance. She wondered what had caused that loud commotion. Suddenly, her own machine began to clink and clang vigorously. She was startled to see all the coins continuously dropping in the bottom of her tray. Filling her bucket, she was elated to have won $250.00 in ten attempts. Deciding not to tempt fate, Mary set out to collect her winnings and quit for the evening. As she waited in line for the cashier, Mary heard someone call her name.

"Are you Mary?" a young-looking waitress asked her.

"Well, yes, I am," Mary said.

"Your daughter asked me to find you and bring you over to her," the waitress replied.

"Is anything the matter?" Mary asked.

"Please come," the waitress insisted.

Mary hurried over to the poker table where Grace was seated. Mary was worried, but she didn't know why. When she arrived, Grace told her to sit down next to her. Noticing the coins in her mother's bucket, Grace asked, "How much did you win?"

"Two hundred and fifty dollars," Mary said. "I was just going to collect when this waitress called me over here. What's going on?"

"Well, I played this new game called **Tri-Poker,**" her daughter said.

"You put three tens down and then you play Poker against the dealer. You get one card at a time. After each card, you get an opportunity to pull back one or two of your tens. However, if you like what you have, you can throw a bonus dollar round at any time before you receive your last card."

Mary could not contain her excitement. "So, what was your first card?"

"A King of Spades," Grace said.

"And your second?"

"A Jack of Spades," Grace said.

"What did you do?" Mary asked.

"I put down the bonus dollar," she said.

"Your third card?" Mary could feel a slight rush surge in her head.

"Ten of Spades," Grace said.

"Did you pull back?" Mary gasped.

"What do you think, Mom? Grace smiled.

"And the fourth card?" Mary could not bear to hear her daughter's answer.

"The Ace of Spades, Mom."

Mary's eyes filled with tears. "Your fifth card was the Queen of Spades," Mary said with certainty.

"Yes, Mom, the Queen. A Royal Flush. Fifty-thousand dollars on a thirty-one dollar bet."

Engulfing her daughter, Mary knew her daughter would never pull back.

And neither would she.

CPSIA information can be obtained at www.ICGtesting.com
Printed in the USA
LVOW061047110112

263251LV00003B/22/P